PASS THE BATON
SUCCESSFUL LEADERSHIP TRANSITION / MARK CONNER

Copyright © 2010 by Mark Conner

Published by Conner Ministries Ltd

Contact:
  WEB: www.markconner.com.au
  Email: mark.conner7@icloud.com

First Edition - September 2006
Second Edition - September 2010
Third Edition - March 2018
This Edition - January 2026

All rights reserved. No part of this publication may be reproduced, stored in a retrieval system, or transmitted in any form or by any means – electronic, mechanical, photocopy, recording, or any other – except for brief quotations in printed reviews, without the prior written consent of the publisher.

Unless otherwise stated, all Scripture quotations are from the Holy Bible, *New International Version*, copyright © 1973, 1978, 1984 by International Bible Society. Used by permission.

Cover design by Matthew H. Deutscher
Oak and Ink Creative
www.oakandink.com

Endorsements for Transforming Your Church

Mark Conner is one of the finest young leaders I know. He is that rare combination of a bright mind and a fully yielded heart. His observations concerning the shifts that must take place in order for a church to reach its redemptive potential are profound. Mark's insights are far more than theory. One visit to his church is all it will take to turn cynics into believers. The Church for the 21st Century will require a higher level of leadership than any other era in human history. Books like this one will contribute a great deal to the development of such leadership. I am deeply grateful to Mark for his friendship and the impact that he is having on churches and leaders in Australia, and increasingly all over the world.

Bill Hybels
Senior Pastor, Willow Creek Community Church

Mark is in my opinion one of the spiritually brightest, organizationally savvy, and theologically intelligent church leaders in Australia today. He has clearly demonstrated great capacity to develop healthy churches in very difficult situations, therefore whatever he says in *Transforming Your Church* has real heft. A worthy read.

Alan Hirsch
Author of *The Shape of Things to Come* and *The Forgotten Ways*

This book is an outstanding tool for every church leader who is serious about seeing growth and fruitfulness in their ministry ... the practical insights will challenge and inspire any believer who longs to be a part of building what Jesus said he would build: his Church!

Brian Houston
Senior Pastor, Hillsong Church

Mark Conner is a superb leader and communicator whose vision has led to remarkable growth in his own church. I am so grateful for his friendship and inspiring example.

Nicky Gumbel
Vicar of Holy Trinity Brompton & Developer of ALPHA International

In this present age, the Church of God must come into the knowledge that it is our time to rise up, be transformed and used by God to fully engage the society and the community that he has placed us in. We are to be the salt and light in our generation! Mark's book will make an important contribution to this end.

Kong Hee
City Harvest Church, Singapore

When Mark speaks I listen. Why? Because Mark is a leader who has grown a dynamic, missional and multicultural church in the soil of post-Christian Melbourne, Australia. He is truly an exceptional voice, who offers advice that is balanced, biblical and brilliant.

Mark Sayers
Author of *The Trouble With Paris* and *The Vertical Self*

Mark's ability to inspire, educate, build and expand the local church is outstanding. A true shepherd with a great ability to communicate will share his rich experience with you in a direct, practical yet visionary way.

Ulf Ekman
Word of Life Church, Sweden

Mark Conner is an outstanding leader who pastors a remarkable church. Both are well on their way to making a great impact for God in the nation of Australia and beyond.

Stuart Robinson
Founding Pastor, Crossway Baptist Church

In this excellent book, Mark Conner has nailed the strategic shifts essential for a church to keep from spilling the revival and harvest coming in the 21st century. Don't miss a point as you go over your ministry and ask yourself the serious questions of change.

Larry Stockstill
Senior Pastor, Bethany World Prayer Center

Transforming Your Church is a book written by a church leader who is a practitioner. He has brought a radical revolution to a very good church, in an effective way. The church is now much larger in numbers through multiplied congregations with a focus on social justice and world-wide missions. This is an essential handbook for those who want to see the local church become centre stage in our world.

Ian Green
Founder of Next Level International & Visionary Leader of Proton

Mark Conner is a leader for today's church. His heritage is rich and his pastoral ministry is graced with wisdom and spiritual discernment. He is a man to be trusted in the coming years.

Frank Damazio
Lead Pastor, City Bible Church, Portland, Oregon

Of all the books I've read on leadership, none is more sensible and helpful, because Mark outlines a clear-headed, practical, step-by-step process of leading your church through change. Read it. Use it with the people on your leadership team.

Gary Kinnaman
Senior Pastor, Word of Grace Church

DEDICATION

I would like to dedicate this book to:

Richard Holland, the founding pastor of CityLife Church (formerly Waverley Christian Fellowship), for his faith, his vision, his enthusiasm, and his continual encouragement to me over many years.

Kevin Conner, my father and the second senior minister of CityLife Church, for his example, his teaching, his love, and for believing in me.

Every Christian leader, that God will give you the courage, the grace and the wisdom to successfully pass the baton to the next generation when the time is right.

SPECIAL THANKS

I would like to give my special thanks to:

My amazing wife Nicole
and our children - Josiah, Natasha and Ashley.
You are the most important people in my life.

Richard Holland and Kevin Conner for contributing many ideas and insights for the content of this book.

The people of CityLife Church – for being willing to take the journey with us over many years and for all the encouragement along the way.

CONTENTS

Opening Words	11
1. Pass the Baton	15
2. Our Story	23
3. Learning from History	31
4. Principles of Successful Leadership Transition	41
5. Leading Your Church Through Change	55
Closing Words	69
Frequently Asked Questions	73
Recommended Reading	85
Postscript	89
Notes	91
Other Resources	95

Opening Words

This book has been written as a response to numerous questions and inquiries about the successful leadership transitions that have taken place at CityLife Church (formerly Waverley Christian Fellowship) in Melbourne, Australia. Over the last four decades, CityLife Church has grown to become a multi-cultural congregation made up of over 9000 people meeting in a variety of locations and times around the city. God's blessing on our church has no doubt been in part because of these effective changes.

Our church was founded in 1967 by Richard Holland who led the church for twenty years. Kevin Conner, my father, became the next senior minister and led the church for the following eight years up until 1994. In 1995, I became the senior minister and I have had the privilege of leading the church since that time.

Opening Words

Amazingly, all three of us have remained in the same church and we have related really well together. Richard passed away on May 12th, 2008 at the ripe old age of eighty-nine. As of the writing of this second edition, my father is eighty-three years of age and still going strong. As for me ... well I am a fair bit younger than that. When Richard was around, he used to enjoy saying, "I was good, Kevin was better but Mark is the best!" So you can see he was a good man to have around.

What a great testimony it is to see a church move from strength to strength through multiple leadership transitions with each leader cheering the other on. People who visit or become a part of our church family often comment on how they feel a sense of solidity, security and safety in the church. I believe that this is the fruit of our successful leadership transitions. Something such as this does not happen by accident. It is a result of the grace of God as well as concerted effort and applied wisdom from church leaders.

In chapter one we will discuss the concept of passing the baton and why it is so important. In chapter two I will present an overview of our story and what God has done in our local church. In chapter three we will glean a few lessons from biblical history and the business world. In chapter four we will consider some important principles for leading successful transitions. Chapter five presents a process for leading change effectively. After some closing words we will answer some frequently asked questions, which I am sure you will find interesting (some may find this the most helpful part of the book). This is followed by some recommended reading for further study.

The focus of this book is on leadership transition within a church environment. However, the principles we will share can be helpful for any leadership transition - whether in the church, in a ministry, in a business or in another organization. This second edition includes updated information, some revised material, as well as reflection questions at the end of each chapter.

It is my privilege to be able to share these insights and thoughts from our journey with you. I pray that they will be an inspiration and a help to you as you pursue the cause of Jesus Christ in our world.

Mark Conner
September 2010

Chapter 1
Pass the Baton

There is no success without a successor and Christianity is always one generation away from extinction. These two sobering facts highlight the urgent need for successful leadership transition in today's churches and ministries. Unless we train up the next generation and pass the baton into their hands, God's purposes could be delayed.

God chooses to reveal himself to individual people and then commissions them to carry out his plan and purpose. Part of their responsibility is to pass on his heart and purposes to their children and the next generation. Like a long relay race, God's purposes have been moving on throughout history right up to our time and they need to continue until Jesus returns again.

Yes, we should live with the preparedness that if Jesus came today we would be ready. However, we must also live with the wisdom and foresight that prepares for the future, in case Jesus does not return in our lifetime. To do anything otherwise would be nothing short of poor stewardship of our place in history.

For example, God chose Abraham and made a covenant with him that included many promises. Some of God's promises were fulfilled in Abraham's lifetime. However, many came to pass after his life was over through his son, Isaac, his grandson, Jacob and the succeeding generations, right through to the time of Jesus and beyond.

In the same way, God has been working in the lives of those who have gone before us. He is now working in and through our lives and he also wants us to play an important role in imparting his purpose and destiny into those who are coming after us. This is what it means to pass the baton.

GOD'S PLAN FOR THE GENERATIONS

In my book, *Transforming Your Church,* I outlined seven strategic shifts that the church needs to make in order to be effective in the 21st century.[1] One of these was a *Generation Shift* where ministry is increasingly passed on by the older generation to the younger. This is not an issue of age (after all, every older person was once a young person and every young person will one day be an older person). It is a matter of building for the future.

The church today faces some major challenges. For instance, many of the largest churches that existed in America twenty years ago are either no longer in existence or have declined significantly. Here in my home country of Australia, there are numbers of churches that are dying or decreasing in numbers. The ones that are growing are realizing the need to reach the next generation with the gospel – our children and our young people.

The prophet Isaiah says that God has "called the generations from the beginning (Isaiah 41:4)." God is carrying out his purposes through the generations of the righteous. We each need to have a sense of destiny in our heart and we must see ourselves as part of the unfolding plan of God throughout the ages of time, not as a separate entity without a past or a future. A study of the Bible reveals that each generation has certain responsibilities before God.[2]

First of all, each generation is to discern and accomplish the will of God for their generation. Every generation is responsible to fulfil God's will for their time in history. We each have a race to run and a role to play in carrying out God's purposes. We must give ourselves to discovering and then passionately pursuing our unique destiny.

> *"For when David had served God's purpose in his own generation, he fell asleep ..." Acts 13:36.*

> *"Now also when I am old and grey-headed, O God, do not forsake me, until I declare your strength to this generation ..." Psalm 71:18.*

The second responsibility of each generation is to rebuild the foundations from past generations. Every generation is responsible to reach back and receive an inheritance from those who have gone before. We did not begin this race; we simply carry it on. We are to build on the truths and experiences of those who have gone before us. Godly people have left us a legacy that we are to build upon. We must discover and value our roots and our heritage.

"Those from among you shall build the old waste places; you shall raise up the foundations of many generations; and you shall be called the Repairer of the Breach, the Restorer of Streets to dwell in." Isaiah 58:12. NKJV

"And they shall rebuild the old ruins, they shall raise up the former desolations, and they shall repair the ruined cities, the desolations of many generations." Isaiah 61:4. NKJV

The third responsibility of each generation is to pass on truth to the next generation and guide them into a personal experience with God. Each generation is responsible to pass the baton of God's purposes on to the next generation. God requires us to leave a heritage and an inheritance for those who follow after us.

"Now also when I am old and grey-headed, O God, do not forsake me, until I declare ... your power to everyone who is to come." Psalm 71:18. NKJV

"We will not hide them from their children, telling to the generation to come the praises of the LORD, and his strength and his wonderful works that he has done." Psalm 78:4. NKJV

GENERATION NEXT

Reaching out to the next generation begins with parents taking the responsibility to teach their children the ways of God, including his commands and principles for living. Christian parents are called to love God with all their heart, obey God's commandments and then impress them on their children through the daily events of life (Deuteronomy 6:1-25). The church also plays an important part in helping to reach children and young people for Christ, then placing in their hearts a sense of purpose and destiny for their lives.

In addition to this, church leaders must also make this *Generation Shift*. Wise, older leaders pass the baton on to the next generation, like Moses did to Joshua. We need older men and women, who are in current leadership positions, to lift to a higher level by becoming spiritual fathers and mothers to a new generation of younger leaders. Leadership transition is vital to the ongoing health and progress of each local church.

Leadership transition needs to happen at every level of leadership and in every area of ministry within the church. We must reach out to and seek to train up the next generation to take ownership and leadership within the local church. If we do not do so, the church has no future.

BE FRUITFUL AND MULTIPLY

God has called each one of us to a fruitful life and ministry (Genesis 1:28. John 15:1-8). However, personal fruitfulness is only one part of God's mandate for our lives. He has also called us to multiply ourselves through the lives of others. True spiritual maturity brings us to a place of reproducing ourselves and making other disciples of Jesus Christ.

Jesus is a prime example of passing the baton. While on earth, he could have done his ministry all by himself but he chose twelve disciples to share the ministry with him. After he ascended back to heaven, he passed the baton on to them. Then he told them to go and do the same with others.

Pass the Baton

The apostle Paul was an outstanding Christian and an excellent minister of the gospel. He had a very fruitful life and ministry. Yet his greatest success was in training up young people like Timothy to carry on the work of the ministry when he was gone. He was able to train other leaders to join him in ministry and thereby multiply his ministry impact. When he wrote to Timothy, he emphasized this need to pass the baton.

> *"You then, my son, be strong in the grace that is in Christ Jesus. And the things you have heard me say in the presence of many witnesses entrust to reliable people who will also be qualified to teach others."* 2 Timothy 2:1-2.

Notice that Paul is firstly concerned that Timothy be strong in his own personal faith. However, he then immediately emphasizes the need for Timothy to pass the baton of ministry on to other faithful people who will be able to pass it on to even more people. Here we have four generations of leaders - Paul, Timothy, reliable leaders and others! Paul was concerned about fruitfulness *and* multiplication of ministry. We are called to do the same.

Whatever your ministry is, you need to intentionally be involved in gathering, motivating, training and mobilizing others into fruitful ministry. This is God's plan – fruitfulness *and* multiplication! Passing the baton is for everyone.

There are two other important strategic shifts that need to take place so that we can see a multiplication of ministries and ministry impact in the church. There is a *Leadership Shift* where church leaders begin to see themselves as equippers, not just ministers. Church leaders need to change their focus from doing ministry themselves to raising up more ministers. A leader needs to take on the role of a coach who empowers others to reach their ministry potential. This is leadership the way

God designed it - equipping and mobilizing others into effective ministry.

Then there is a *Ministry Shift* where the members of the congregation begin to see themselves as contributors not just consumers. God has a vision, a dream and a destiny for each individual person and this includes a significant contribution to the local church and the world around them.[3]

The harvest is huge. The need is great. What we need are more willing workers to get involved in the work of the ministry. Let's pray and believe for God to use the leaders of today's church to disciple many people into effective ministry.

Jesus did not suggest that we should pray for a bigger task or a larger harvest field, as if the Great Commission is not challenging enough. He told us to pray for more labourers. We need more people who will take up the challenge of working for the expansion of the kingdom of God on earth (Matthew 9:36-38).

REFLECTION QUESTIONS

1. What comes to your mind when you hear the phrase "pass the baton?"

2. Reflect on the statement, "Christianity is always one generation from extinction." Is that true and, if so, what are the implications?

3. What steps can we take to fully lay hold of the heritage and inheritance available to us from those who have lived before our time?

4. God's original mandate for humanity was to be fruitful *and* to multiply. What are some of the reasons why we tend to focus only on personal fruitfulness?

5. What are some of the barriers (practically, mentally and emotionally) to passing the baton on to others?

6. God's design for his *leaders* is for them to be equippers of others and to release them into ministry. Why do you think many church leaders fail to empower others?

7. God's design for his *people* is for them to be actively involved in his work on earth. What are some of the challenges of helping people to break out of a consumer mindset?

8. Imagine your church or your ministry fifty years from now. What could it look like? What are some of the key factors that will shape that picture?

Chapter 2
Our Story

GOOD FOUNDATIONS (1967-1987)

Chapter 1 of our story began back in 1967 under the leadership of our founding pastor, Richard Holland. Waverley Mission, as our church was originally called, started officially in a small rented shop front on Glenwood Avenue in an eastern suburb in Melbourne, Australia, called Glen Waverley. The church began with eight families.

The worship, the Bible teaching and the fellowship were enjoyed by all. In the short space of two years time the church grew to over one hundred people. The ten by six metre room soon became too small so the church moved to another venue, then another and then another as the church family continued to grow to over three hundred people.[4]

Richard believed that God had called the church to reach more people and so they began looking for land – something large that would meet all of our future needs – 10 acres. Soon 9.6 acres were found on High Street Road in Wantirna South (further out in the eastern suburbs of Melbourne). The purchase price was $250,000, a seemingly insurmountable amount for the church at the time. An amount of $205,000 was offered and the seller accepted.

Through the sale of a property owned by the church and some other funds that had been put aside, the land was paid for but then a new building was going to cost approximately $600,000. As senior minister at that time, Richard felt overwhelmed and even sick in his stomach for over two months. But as he prayed he sensed the Lord impressing on him very strongly, "The money is in the church!" So the vision was shared and the members of the church gave $200,000, loaned $200,000 interest-free and the remaining $200,000 was loaned from the bank then paid off in three years.

In 1983, a new church building was opened and dedicated, seating up to 800 people. This new auditorium included a kitchen, multiple offices, an audio-visual room, a large foyer, a bookshop, Sunday school rooms and two other meeting rooms. Due to the death of its senior pastor, Parkmore Full Gospel Church merged with Waverley Christian Fellowship at this time. The church also inherited a small Christian school which was renamed Waverley Christian College.

In this twenty-year period (1967-1986), the church grew to over 500 people attending each weekend. In addition to many families and single people, numbers of university students from other countries became part of the church during this time. No doubt, this was an early catalyst to the future multi-cultural nature of the church.

Richard's ministry was characterized by enthusiasm, friendliness, evangelism, hospitality, genuine love for people and faith to believe God for the miraculous. Many people became part of our church during Chapter 1. This chapter is filled with many good memories.[5]

BUILDING A HOUSE FOR GOD (1987-1994)

After twenty years of being the senior minister, Richard passed the baton of leadership to my father, Kevin Conner. This occurred in September, 1986. My dad had been assisting Richard with the leadership of the church for a number of years before this time, beginning in 1981 when our family returned from a season of living in the USA.

By early 1987, Chapter 2 of our church's story was starting to be written, under the leadership of my dad.[6] It was new chapter, a little different, but building on the foundations that had already been laid. The church continued to grow and reach more and more people in the local community and beyond. The worship, teaching and fellowship continued to be enjoyed by all and a larger core of committed people were being raised up.

Eventually two Sunday morning church meetings were started, which led to a second stage to the original building. This included a new auditorium seating 1,250 people which was opened in 1994. This was the largest project the church had ever embarked on. It required a lot of hard work and sacrificial giving.

These were days of prayer, great sacrifice in time, money and talents, and many "working bees." Richard Holland's son-in-law, Pier Van Netten, went for one year without pay to oversee the construction of the church building. In fact, he invoiced the church for the grand total of $1.00, a bill which we finally paid just a few years ago! A friend of mine, David Croft, who was twenty years old at that time, laid 70,000 bricks all by himself, save one (Richard laid the last one!). The stories could go on and on about how people worked diligently and gave generously to build a home that would reach more people for Christ.

My dad's leadership during this time was characterized by excellent teaching, establishing order and structure, and equipping people in the Word of God. Many people became part of our church during Chapter 2. During this time the church grew to over 1,000 people attending each Sunday morning, with about 1,600 people calling it their church home.

FURTHER EXPANSION (1995 - ?)

After eight years of being the Senior Minister, Kevin Conner passed the baton of leadership to me in February, 1995. Two chapters were finished, filled with stories of love, joy, spiritual growth, life change, as well as the normal challenges, during almost thirty years of building and expansion. Chapter 3 was new chapter, a little different again, but once again built on the strong foundations already laid by those who had gone before.

A lot has happened in the last fifteen years. There has been further expansion and growth and many more people have been impacted by the life of our church. Many people have become part of our church during this time.[7]

Here are some of the highlights:

- We have articulated a clear mission statement and a list of core values for our church.[8]

- Our church currently has an average of over 5,500 different people attending eleven meetings in five different locations across Melbourne each weekend. This includes a church plant in Hobson's Bay led by Ted and Solveig Fabiyanic with two locations. The other congregations are functioning as a multi-site church being "one church in multiple locations." This includes four weekend church meetings at our location in the suburb of Knox, a Sunday morning gathering in the suburb of Casey, two Sunday morning gatherings in the suburb of Manningham, as well as church meetings at Knox for Chinese people and at Casey for Spanish speaking people.[9]

- Our church has a network of over 500 small groups, called Life Groups, where people meet for fellowship, care, discipleship and outreach in different locations all across the city.[10]

- CityLife Church is a very diverse community of people, with over 110 nationalities represented. This reflects the highly cosmopolitan nature of the city of Melbourne.

- We created LIFETRAX, which is our life and leadership development program. It has helped disciple, train and equip thousands of people in the life of our church, mobilizing many of them into ministry and/or leadership.[11]

- Our generation ministries to children, youth, young adults and seniors are healthy and growing.

- Our local community ministry, CityLife Community Care, provides low cost counselling and a wide variety of programs to meet community needs at our various locations around the city of Melbourne.

- Our Christian school, Waverley Christian College, has over 1,200 students. In addition to establishing spiritual and moral values in the hearts of the students, the academic standard of the school is very high, with graduating students scoring in the top 7% of all students in the State of Victoria.

- Our World Impact mission ministry is involved in strategic activities in many nations. This includes church planting, short term teams and partnering with other key local ministries.

- A wide variety of other ministries are actively carrying out our mission to "raise up fervent followers of Jesus Christ who will reach out and impact communities, cities and nations for the kingdom of God."

- In 2002, we crafted a Vision 2010 statement to guide the church over this eight year period (2002 - 2010). This statement included quantitative goals for the main ministries of the church. It has served us well, creating greater alignment across our ministries and helping us to take seriously our mission as a church. For 2011 onwards, we are moving towards a more qualitative focus.

- In 2004, we completed a major building expansion at our Knox campus that cost seven million dollars. We were able to complete this debt free through the generous donations of our church members. Our expanded auditorium seats 2,000 people and we have been able to upgrade many other parts of our building so as to better serve people.

- At the opening of our expanded facilities in October 2004, we changed our church name from Waverley Christian Fellowship to CityLife Church. The reason for this is because we are no longer located in the suburb of Waverley and also to reflect our vision to bring God's life to the wider city of Melbourne.

- The leadership structures of the church have been modified a number of times as the church has grown over the last fifteen years. A few years back we conducted an extensive governance review of the church and all of its ministries. This resulted in a number of key changes.

- In 2007 we celebrated our fortieth anniversary as a church. What a joy it was to see three different senior ministers who love and support each other still in the same church. This is a very unique thing for which we are truly grateful. As mentioned earlier, Richard Holland passed away in 2008.

Our church has been blessed with leaders who have been secure enough to let others rise, to pass on the baton, and to build something that would last beyond themselves. These are godly people who were not into building a kingdom for themselves. They were committed to expanding the kingdom of God, even if it meant them stepping aside or into another role in order to see another generation arise.

Someone once said, "Richard was the founder and gatherer, Kevin was the builder and establisher and Mark is the entrepreneur and extender." We are thankful for over four decades of ongoing blessing and growth because of successful leadership transition. Without Chapter 1, there would be no Chapter 2 and without

Chapter 1 and 2 there would be no Chapter 3. Today we all benefit because of the efforts and sacrifice of those who have gone before. Previous generations left a legacy for us and we will have the opportunity to do the same for others.

What is most exciting is that we believe some of our best years are ahead. More of Chapter 3 is yet to be written and there may be more chapters yet to come as the next generation emerges to lay hold of God's purposes.

REFLECTION QUESTIONS

1. What stood out to you most from the CityLife story?

2. Outline the history of your own church or ministry. What clear chapters do you see? What patterns emerge? What lessons can you glean?

3. What lessons can you glean from the CityLife story that could be applied into your situation?

4. What are some of unique contributions that a ministry founder or church planter make?

5. What are some of the unique aspects of inheriting a church or ministry you did not start?

6. Most people groups or organizations have a *life cycle* of some sort, starting with birth and ending in death or closure. What can we do to ensure our churches or ministries have as long a life as possible?

7. What are some of the benefits of studying other churches or ministries?

Chapter 3
Learning from History

It was once said, "The only thing we learn from history is that we never learn from history!" It is very easy to make the same mistakes as those made by previous generations or to fail to learn from the positive example of those who have walked wisely before God. What a sad reality.

When King Charles II of Spain died in 1701 with no heir, the result was the War of Spanish Succession. This war entangled France, England, Italy, Austria, and the Netherlands in a conflict that lasted thirteen years. In the same way, failure to plan for succession in churches may result in stagnation, or as Spain discovered, serious conflict.[12]

Before we take time to glean some lessons from our local church story, we want to take a few moments to have a quick survey of a number of other leadership transitions. There is much we can learn from the experience of others. Let's consider some insights from both biblical times and from our contemporary world.

GETTING IT RIGHT

God chose Abraham and gave him many promises regarding his life and that of his children (Genesis 12:1-7; 13:14-17; 15:5, 13-21; 17:1-16). The Lord said about Abraham, "For I have chosen him, so that he will direct his children and his household after him to keep the way of the LORD by doing what is right and just, so that the LORD will bring about for Abraham what he has promised him (Genesis 18:19)." Although Abraham was far from perfect, he served God faithfully and he was faithful in passing on the ways of God to his son Isaac and to his grandchildren. God's covenant promises and requirements were passed on successfully to the following generations.

Moses was called by God to lead the nation of Israel out of Egypt and into the Promised Land in fulfilment of the covenant promises given to Abraham many generations earlier. Unfortunately, Moses never entered the land but only saw it from a distance. God told him to appoint Joshua as his successor and the one who would lead Israel into the future. Moses trained Joshua as his assistant and gradually transferred responsibility and authority to him (Exodus 24:13; 33:11). Eventually Moses died and Joshua led the next generation into the land of Canaan (Joshua 1:1-2).

David was a man after God's own heart and he was chosen to be king in place of Saul who had lost the anointing through disobedience (1 Samuel 13:14). David had it in his heart to build God a house. However, because he had been a man of war, God told him that he was not the one to do this, even though it was a noble intention. David's son, Solomon, was to be his successor and would be the one to build a magnificent house for God. David prepared well for the transition of leadership to his son Solomon and he gathered many materials in advance for the building of the temple, including a large generous donation from his own personal wealth (1 Chronicles 28-29. 1 Kings 5:1-6).

Near the end of his ministry, the Lord told the prophet Elijah to anoint Elisha as his successor. Elijah did so and Elisha served Elijah faithfully until Elijah was taken up to heaven. A double portion of Elijah's anointing was passed on to Elisha and he did twice as many miracles as his mentor (1 Kings 19:15-21. 2 Kings 2:1-18).

The book of Esther tells the story of Mordecai looking after and raising his young cousin, Esther, after both of her parents had died. She rose from being an unknown Jewish girl to become queen of the mighty Persian Empire. Through Mordecai's motivation she seized the moment and used her influence to save her people from a sinister plot from Haman, who was trying to wipe out the Jewish people (see the Book of Esther).

Although John the Baptist struggled somewhat with his understanding of Jesus' ministry (Matthew 11:1-6), he recognized that his primary role was that of a forerunner to prepare the way for the ministry of Jesus (Matthew 3:1-6; 4:12-17). After Jesus' ministry started, John then faded into the background. He is an example of someone who let go well, accepting the need for Jesus' profile and prominence to increase while his decreased (John 3:22-36).

We have already seen that Jesus did an excellent job passing on ministry to his disciples. He gave them a huge mandate to take the gospel to the entire world (Matthew 28:18-20). He not only motivated them, he also equipped them with all that they needed to fulfil their God-given mission.

As we mentioned earlier, the apostle Paul trained many younger leaders such as Timothy and Titus. He invested much of his time motivating and equipping other church leaders to be true to the faith and to be effective in ministry. He then expected them to pass on what they had learned from him to another generation of leaders so that the work of the church would continue to expand (2 Timothy 2:1-2).

In each of these cases we see a leader who realized the importance of passing the baton and a successor who took his or her calling seriously. As a result, God's purposes were carried out from generation to generation. This is the way God intends it to be.

GETTING IT WRONG

Joshua was an outstanding leader. He took the baton of leadership from his mentor, Moses. He then ran an incredible race himself, serving his generation by helping them take possession of the entire Promised Land. He motivated his own generation to serve God all the days of his life, and the lives of the other leaders who outlived him. But Joshua failed to do one important task. He failed to pass the baton on to the next generation. He did not train a successor. After Joshua died, there arose another generation, who did not know the Lord and, as a result, the entire nation of Israel drifted from God's purposes for many years (Joshua 24:31. Judges 2:7-15).

Eli was the last of the judges and he was also a priest given the responsibility for God's house. However, due to his failure to discipline his sons, he lost the lineage of God's blessing and was judged severely by God. Both he and his sons were killed (1 Samuel 1-4). God's final judgment against Eli and his descendants occurred when Solomon removed Abiathar, Eli's descendant, and put Zadok in his place as high priest of the nation of Israel (1 Kings 2:35).

Under the leadership of Solomon, the nation of Israel reached the height of its prosperity and influence. Tragically, in his latter years Solomon's heart turned away from God and after his death the kingdom was divided into two because of leadership conflict. This was primarily because his son, Rehoboam, refused to listen to the wise advice of his elders (1 Kings 12:1-17). The majority of the kings of both Israel and Judah were wicked and led God's people astray resulting in both kingdoms being taken into captivity by foreign empires, with only the southern kingdom of Judah ever returning to her land.

Elisha the prophet picked up Elijah's mantle and inherited a double portion of his spiritual father's anointing. However, his assistant, Gehazi, failed to inherit the ministry blessing. This was because of personal character flaws, including greed, lying and the misuse of the prophetic office. He ended up cursed with leprosy (2 Kings 5).

In each of these cases we see either a leader who failed to select and train a successor OR a potential successor who failed to lay hold of God's calling for their life. The tragic result was the dropping of the baton and many seemingly lost years. What a tragedy.

LET'S GET SMART

In the context of talking about business and financial management, Jesus once said, "… the people of this world are more shrewd in dealing with their own kind than are the people of the light (Luke 16:8)." This was not a compliment! This truth is still the same today - people in the business world are often smarter and more passionate about being successful and making a profit than people in the church are about fulfilling the mission God has given them. This should not be so.

Here is an example of some wisdom from the business world that confirms our need to make successful leadership transitions in the church.

- Jim Collins in his best-selling book *Built to Last*, shares his research from studying a number of companies that had lasted for multiple decades.[13] All of them had leaders that were able to build an organization that would last well beyond them. Their greatest achievement was the creation of the organization itself, including its mission and values, not their personal accomplishments.

- Many successful CEOs in today's businesses start their search for a prospective successor many years in advance. For example, Jack Welch began preparing and grooming potential successors at General Electric seven years before he intended on retiring. Out of 225,000 workers in 1993, he identified twenty potential successors; over seven years, he reduced the number to three before one was finally chosen.

- In his article "Ending the CEO Succession Crisis," Ram Charan says that all companies must do three things: (1) have available a deep pool of internal candidates kept well stocked by a leadership development process,[14] (2) ensure that the Board of Directors has an updated succession plan and a thoughtful process in place for making decisions about candidates, and (3) ensure that any consideration of outside candidates is done in a thorough and exacting manner.[15]

- Bob Joy, senior vice president of global human resources for Colgate-Palmolive says, "If you start five years or even ten years before the CEO is going to retire, it may be too late."[16]

- Kenneth W. Freeman in his article on "The CEOs Real Legacy" says this in regard to CEO succession planning: "Begin early, look first inside your company for exceptional talent, see that candidates gain experience in all aspects of the business and help them develop the skills they'll need in the top job."[17] He encourages the existing CEO to take the initiative in thinking about succession rather than waiting for the Board to raise the issue. He urges CEOs to: not see their roles as permanent, to break through the ego problem and be willing to let go of the helm at the right time, to not just look for candidates that resemble them but ones that can take the company into the future, and to see that their true legacy is what happens to the company after they leave.

Without doubt, the church environment has many differences to the world of business. However, in the area of leadership succession, if business leaders can think and plan ahead so that their businesses have the greatest potential of being profitable over the long haul, how much more should church and ministry leaders do the same so that the cause of Jesus Christ continues to advance in our world. Do not do so is an abdication of one of our crucial God-given responsibilities: to pass the baton.

START A NEW GENERATION

Maybe you are in a situation where passing the baton has not gone well or has been non-existent. Maybe you have inherited a church where the transition was not that ideal. Thankfully, we can start a new generation. No matter what our pervious leaders were or are like, we can begin to serve God with all of our hearts today and carry his purposes forward.

Many people have risen to achieve their life purpose even under people that were not godly. The prophet Samuel developed an intimate relationship with God in a time of apostasy and under a leader who compromised his standards. God shaped the heart and character of David under the leadership of King Saul who had lost the anointing and was jealous of young David.

My own father, Kevin Conner, was an unwanted child who grew up in foster homes for boys and he never met his natural parents. Yet he was able to start a new godly generation by serving God himself and then raising my sister and me to serve the Lord. Now, we have the responsibility to do our best to train up others to serve God fully.

My dad also experienced a number of ministry environments in his early years that were unhealthy and dysfunctional and yet he was able to learn from them and appropriate those lessons in helping to extend the purposes of God in our church.[18] Remember, we can always learn something wherever we are placed – sometimes what *to* do and sometimes what *not* to do.

You are not a victim of circumstances or a product of only your environment. By the grace of God, you can rise above any situation and lay hold of God and his purpose for your life. Let's learn from history and from the business world, and then start writing an even better history right here right now. Let's start a new generation!

REFLECTION QUESTIONS

1. It is easy to neglect the lessons we can learn from history. What are some steps you could take to become more of a student of how God has worked in the past?

2. The apostle Paul tells us that everything written in the Bible was done so for our learning. What are some of the benefits we can glean from studying leaders God used in biblical times?

3. Reflect on the ministry of Joshua. He was such an outstanding leader. What do you think were some of the contributing factors to him not raising up a successor?

4. Reflect on John the Baptist and his ministry. What sort of feelings and emotions may he have had as his ministry started to fade and Jesus' ministry started to emerge and gather momentum?

5. Is it appropriate for followers of Christ to learn from the business world? What similarities are there between a business and a church congregation? What differences are there?

6. What other churches or ministries can you think of in terms of leadership transition? What insights can you glean from the situations that were positive and went well? What lessons can you learn from transitions that were poor or unsuccessful?

7. What steps can we take to ensure we learn from others and not repeat some of the same mistakes?

Chapter 4
Principles of Successful Leadership Transition

TRANSITION TIME

In any relay race, the passing of the baton is a crucial time that can make or break the team's success. Letting go too soon or holding on too long can spell disaster. It takes a lot of skill and wisdom to pass the baton successfully in any race, including leadership succession. That is what this book is about.

In the 1981 Olympics, the Olympic Torch was relayed across the United States of America by the hand of 4,000 runners. Each had to make the transition of the torch from their hand to another person's hand. The torch was relayed all the way from New York to Los Angeles. No one dropped the torch. All 4,000 runners were in Los Angeles as the last runner came in with the torch and lit the flame.

What a challenge for the church of Jesus Christ to do the same as the torch of the gospel is passed on through the generations, from leader to leader. No doubt God wants us to make successful transitions. He does not want us to drop the baton.[19]

Let's now look at a number of practical principles of successful leadership transition. We will speak specifically about transition from one senior minister to another in a local church context but these principles apply to any leadership transition, whether it is in a ministry or other organisational setting.

1. CHOOSE YOUR SUCCESSOR CAREFULLY

The selection of a successor is a very important decision. It needs to be undertaken with much prayer and consideration. Proper attention needs to be given to the character, the competency and the cultural compatibility of the potential future leader.

Like any leadership role, the role of senior minister in a church, requires a wide variety of ministry skills and experience. These need to be considered when selecting a potential successor.[20] Some of the spiritual gifts that are essential in any growing church include leadership, teaching, wisdom and faith.

Each church has a unique decision-making process. In our church, the current senior minister has had the freedom to nominate their successor. However, a decision of this magnitude also requires confirmation from our Board of Elders. The members of our congregation must also affirm any nomination of a new senior minister.

In 1986, our founding pastor, Richard Holland, nominated my father, Kevin Conner, as his successor. Richard had experienced a number of health challenges that were the catalyst for this decision. My dad had been assisting Richard for quite a few years and therefore already had good rapport with the people. He had also been on the leadership team of Bible Temple in Portland, Oregon with Dick Iverson from 1972-1981. These years had given him much experience in the environment of a large growing church. After Richard's nomination, the elders and the congregation confirmed the appointment of my father as senior minister.

In 1993, at the age of 66, my father nominated me as his successor, not because I was his natural son but because he believed that I had the calling and ability to lead the church forward. I had been a part of the church staff team for eight years and had gained experience in a wide variety of ministries, including worship, youth, administration, pastoral care and preaching. The elders and the congregation confirmed my appointment as senior minister.

During both of these leadership transitions, the church did not lose any people but rather continued to move from strength to strength. Yes, there were changes and adjustments that had to be made due to the unique personality and spiritual gifting of each senior minister. No, not everyone found it easy to make these adjustments and before and after these transitions people did move on for various reasons, as in any church community. However, there was general unity around the need for change and the selection of the appropriate leader.

There are many benefits in choosing a successor from *within* the local church. The prospective leader has been observed firsthand, their strengths and weaknesses are well known, they understand the history and culture of church, and they have had the opportunity to build good rapport and relationships with the people in the church. If they have the leadership gifting required to take the church forward, rather than just maintain the status quo, then an internal leader may be the ideal successor. This approach is also most likely to be the least disruptive for the church.

Occasionally, there may not be anyone internally who has the experience or potential to be a successor. In this case, someone from *outside* the church may be the best choice for this role. Obviously, their character and ministry competency need to be affirmed, as already mentioned. However, one of the most important things to consider is what could be called "cultural fit."

The *culture* of a church is a composite of the history, the traditions and the personality of a church congregation. It describes what it feels like to be part of a particular church and how things are done in that environment. Culture is often unspoken but it is very influential. A godly gifted person may fail as a successor simply because they simply do not fit the culture of the church and therefore the local body rejects them as a transplant. Yes, the ideal successor will bring change to any church culture but unless they can first fit within and connect to the existing culture then it will be unlikely that they will be successful in leading the church forward.

Before appointing a successor from outside of the church it is wise to arrange a number of visits, ministry opportunities and relational experiences between the church, the existing leaders and the potential successor before committing to a final decision. It is somewhat similar to going out together for a while before becoming engaged and eventually married. The greater the required commitment and the higher the potential risk in any new relationship, the more important it is to take your time and prayerfully consider all aspects of whether your future together has a strong foundation.

Each of the following principles is important but selecting the right person is crucial. Be patient and avoid making a hasty decision. Pray and ask God to direct you and show you his will. Consider multiple options. Observe potential successors in different environments and ministry situations, especially under pressure. There will always be some degree of risk. You can never guarantee the future but you can make a decision that is characterized by wisdom and the leading of the Holy Spirit.

2. ENSURE THAT THE MISSION CONTINUES

God has a purpose for his church and he carries this out through the generations of the righteous. Wise church leaders build their churches to last well beyond their time. They create a sense of mission and values that will continue on even when they are gone.[21]

Although we have had three senior ministers now, the mission and the values of our church have continued through each season. Yes, leadership style, ministry emphasis and church programs have changed along the way. However, the foundations have remained the same as the church has continued to grow under different leadership.

In considering a successor, do not just look for any competent leader. Look for someone who believes in God's unique calling for your church. You need someone who is committed to bringing that mission into further reality.[22]

Moses passed the baton of leadership on to Joshua. The leadership was different but the mission was still the same – taking the people of Israel into the Promised Land. David passed the baton of leadership to his son Solomon. The leadership was different but the vision was still the same - building God a glorious house.

Principles of Successful Leadership Transition

Richard had a vision of a church of 1,500 people influencing the local community. Although he did not see this happen under his leadership, he was to see this come to pass through his successors. My father had specific things that God spoke to him about for our church and its future. Some of them he saw happen under his leadership while others have happened since he passed on the baton. In many ways, like David, my dad had a vision for God's house but it turned out to be his son, in our case me (like Solomon) that was privileged to bring it into reality.

The incoming leader needs to see themselves not as starting their own race or doing their own thing – leading the church off in any direction they want. They need to see themselves as the next runner in the race, building on the progress that has already been made by those who have gone before and then carrying the purposes of God forward.

I see our church as belonging to God. It is his, not mine. Jesus is the Head of the church therefore its primary leader. Being a good leader first means learning to be a good follower. The apostle Paul once said, "Follow me as I follow Christ (1 Corinthians 11:1)." I have the privilege of overseeing this current season in the life of our church. I desire to hear God's voice and carry out his will for our church to the very best of my ability, then be ready to let go and pass the baton on to the next leader, at the appropriate time.

As you consider a potential successor, think about the mission and the values that are important to you and your church. Articulate them clearly and then look for a successor who is committed to preserving them as well as passionately leading the church forward. Yes, the mission and the values may be fine-tuned, further clarified and even expanded over time, but the overall direction should ideally remain the same. Otherwise a lot of damage is done by successive leaders steering the congregation in all sorts of different directions.

3. KNOW THE RIGHT TIMING

In a relay race, the successful passing of the baton requires excellent timing. Knowing the right person to pass the baton on to is important but effectively making the actual transition at the right time is vital. That is where success or failure often occurs.

Avoid seeking to pass the leadership baton on too soon. Otherwise you may not maximise your own contribution to the race and/or the next leader may not be up to speed yet. The result is lost momentum. On the other hand, avoid hanging on to the baton for too long. This will also result in a loss of momentum.

It is sad to see ministers hold on to their leadership positions until they die or until the church plateaus or declines. This is not God's will. Every leader should look for his or her successor well in advance. Failing to pass on the baton soon enough can also frustrate potential leaders who are ready to run but feel like they will never have an opportunity. This is why some young leaders leave the church prematurely.

In both of our leadership transitions the timing worked well. Richard had experienced some health problems. My dad was already very active ministering alongside Richard so when the decision was made the change took place and all went relatively smoothly. The timing was right for Richard, for the church and for my dad.

My dad was 66 years of age when he nominated me as his successor. When my dad had turned 68 years of age the official transition took place and I was inaugurated as the senior minister of our church. I was 33 years of age at the time. The timing was right for my dad, for the church and for me as a young leader.[23] It worked well and the church went from strength to strength.

4. ESTABLISH A CLEAR TRANSITION PROCESS

So far we have spoken about choosing the right person, ensuring that the mission carries on and knowing the right timing. Next, it is important to consider the actual transition process.

In a relay race there is a time when both runners are in the exchange zone and there are a few moments when both of them are holding the baton together before one lets go and the other takes off on their own. This is a crucial part of the race and therefore you want to do all you can to get this right. In most races, this is where the team can lose time and position, or even be disqualified.

The transition from Richard to my dad occurred quite quickly due to Richard's health situation. In August of 1986, this decision was confirmed by our church members and then on September 7th of that same year my dad was set in as the new senior minister with everyone's full support.[24]

In contrast, there was a two year transition period between my dad's and my leadership of the church. During this time I began doing all of the day-to-day running of the church but my dad was still the senior minister. However, everyone knew that at the end of this two year period I would be given the leadership of the church.

This was a very important time and it helped people to gradually adjust to the idea of me becoming the senior leader. It also helped my dad begin to gradually let go of his previous ministry role and it helped me to start to pick up speed in my preparation to be ready to take the lead role. In our situation, a two year transition time was ideal. One year would have been too quick and three years would have been too long.

In determining your own transition process and timing, consider all of the various factors – the age, effectiveness and energy level of the current leader, the age and ministry experience of the successor, as well as the congregation's response to all of this.

In our case, Richard stayed in the church after he passed the baton to my dad. To help him let go emotionally and to give my dad some space to establish his own leadership, Richard chose to engage in some travelling ministry for a number of months. My dad also did the same after I became the senior minister. This was an important part of the success of our leadership transitions.

Usually, when a new senior minister is appointed, the previous senior minister relocates to another church. There are good reasons for this and at times this is the ideal arrangement. However, our situation has been unique and by God's grace we have been able to navigate the potential tensions that can arise when previous senior ministers remain (more about this later).

5. MAKE A DECISION TO LET GO

As the transition concludes it is essential that the previous leader fully let go of the baton and allow the new leader appropriate freedom to fulfil their role. When the previous leader leaves the congregation and relocates to another church or ministry, this is somewhat easy. When the previous leader stays in the same congregation, this can be quite difficult. It is essential that they not seek to exercise remote control or in any way undermine the new leader. They must give the new leader their full support and backing. If this does not happen then the new leader will feel frustrated and hindered in their leadership role, which is never God's will.

By God's grace, we have been able to see our church move forward without any major conflict between current and previous senior ministers. A big part of this achievement has been both Richard and my father choosing to let go appropriately.

In our situation, both leadership transitions were initiated by the existing leader. No one was trying to push Richard or my dad out of leadership. They recognized the need for change and had the courage to make it happen.

This takes a good deal of godly character and, as my dad calls it, *internal security*. If a leader's sense of value, worth and significance is overly tied to their leadership position or ministry title, then they will be hesitant to let go or make a change. In contrast, secure leaders realize that their value, worth and significance come from who they are, not from what they do or the position they hold. Therefore, they are willing to let go for the benefit of others and the church itself. When this happens, outgoing leaders only gain more credibility and honour.

True spiritual fathers (and mothers) long to see their children rise and do better than they have. Part of this is being willing to pass on to others what they have worked so hard for. That is not an easy task but it can be done.

Further along, when the transition is well over, previous leaders need to continue to let go, realizing that changes will be made. Some of those changes will likely require grace to handle. This is especially so when the new leader does things differently than they would have done.

Previous leaders should focus on their new season of ministry, seeking to make a continuing contribution in their areas of calling. They can also provide advice and input when requested. They should be able to look back with a sense of fulfilment that they have run their senior leadership race well and that they will be well rewarded. Ultimately, each local church is in God's hands and he will continue to watch over its well being.

6. UNDERSTAND THE IMPORTANCE OF HONOUR

For incoming leaders, it is essential to honour those who have gone before. We do not worship the past but we should honour it and recognise that we would not be where we are today without the sacrifices and contribution of earlier generations. We have received an inheritance and a heritage that others have worked hard for.

To honour someone means to treat them with value and to esteem them highly. My father always endeavoured to honour Richard for his twenty years of pioneering our church. Richard and my dad had unity of vision but had very different personalities, different spiritual gifts and different styles of ministry. It required a great deal of grace for both of them to stick together and it required adjustment along the way but they always endeavoured to honour each other.

I have always tried to honour both Richard and my father for the foundations they laid in our church. I did not start our church. I had the privilege of inheriting a church that I did not found or build. My personality, spiritual gifts and ministry style are different than my dad's and Richard's. However, despite this, we have always tried to respect and honour each other as persons and to be united around the ongoing mission of the church.

Although our focus as a church is on the future and the vision God has for us, at regular times we stop and reflect on where we have come from, including giving honour to those who have gone before and made possible what is happening today. When we honour previous leaders it makes it easier for them to let go. When they let go it makes it easier for the new leader to keep honouring. The result is an upward spiral of mutual respect and appreciation. The opposite is also true. When new leaders fail to honour previous leaders it makes it much harder for them to let go. When they do not let go, it is easy for the new leader to stop honouring. The result is a downward spiral of underlying tensions that become detrimental for everyone involved, including the church.

The past was not perfect, nor were previous leaders just like the present is not perfect nor is the current leader. However, we can focus on the positive aspects of church life and ministry. We can also express appreciation for what we have inherited.

In the transition from my dad to me, I did not see this as my dad *stepping down* or even *stepping aside*. You do not fire fathers. Fathers become grandfathers and continue to fulfil an important role in the wider family environment. I viewed our transition as my dad *stepping up* into doing more of the ministry activities that he alone could do and being released from ministry tasks that others like myself could do.

My dad stayed on our staff team for many years. We agreed on a job description that enabled him to make contributions in the areas of his strengths. He has taught in our various training courses, he continues to write books, he travels and ministers in other nations and he gives input to a fellowship of ministers that look to him as a spiritual father. He has been busier since retiring as the senior minister of our church than he was before. My dad continues to make a valuable contribution to our church and to the wider body of Christ. Richard did the same right through to the end of his time with us.

For a variety of reasons, not every leadership transition is successful. Change does not always go as we intend it to. However, we should do everything that we can to see that transitions work out for the best – for the benefit of God's people, for the continuation of God's purposes and for the honour of God's name.

[See the Frequently Asked Questions section later in the book for a variety of other transition ideas and insights]

REFLECTION QUESTIONS

1. Reflect on the metaphor of a *relay race*. In what way is leadership transition similar? In what way is it different?

2. Is it always appropriate for a leader to choose their own successor? In what situations would it not be? What are some of the advantages and disadvantages of a leader choosing their successor?

3. Should the *mission* of a church or ministry be open to review and change? If so, in what situations?

4. How important is *timing* in leadership transition? What are some of the factors that contribute to determining the appropriate time for change?

5. Consider the *transition process*. What is an appropriate length of time and what needs to take place during this process?

6. What are some of the contributing factors to a leader finding it difficult to *let go*? What can be done to overcome these?

7. How can we *honour* the past without worshipping it?

8. When the past has had more negative that positive aspects, what can a new leader do to handle this kind of situation appropriately?

Chapter 5
Leading Your Church Through Change

I believe that leading change is one of the most important yet challenging tasks of any leader. Everything else is somewhat easy in comparison, whether it is preaching, team building, counselling or providing pastoral care. Leading change demands the best of our prayer, wisdom, pastoral sensitivity and courage.

God calls every church leader to be a *change agent* who leads his or her people forward to greater effectiveness in achieving their mission and impacting their community, city and other nations. Like Israel, God wants his church to "break camp and advance" and to quit going around the same mountain over and over (Deuteronomy 1:6-8; 2:1-3). Yes, we have come a long way but there is more to be done and more progress to be made. In fact, unless you keep changing and growing your church will eventually plateau or decline.[25]

If you are a new leader in a church situation, it is inevitable that there will be aspects of church life and ministry that will need to change. Knowing *what* to change is very important. However, knowing *how* to lead that change is just as important.

In my first year as the senior minister of our church, I sensed God speak to me about seven strategic changes or shifts that we needed to make in our church. These emerged out of a time of personal prayer and Bible study, as well as from observations of other growing churches.[26] I knew clearly *what* needed to change.

What I needed next was a model or process for *how* to lead change effectively. God spoke to me from the life of Nehemiah. The apostle Paul tells us that the stories recorded in the Old Testament were written for our learning and benefit (1 Corinthians 10:11). As I read the narrative of Nehemiah's life I gleaned a number of principles for leading change effectively. Here is a brief summary of them:[27]

1. SEE THE NEED FOR CHANGE

Nehemiah was working in a comfortable job in the palace of a foreign king. He received a report from his homeland, Israel, about the terrible condition of his people and their capital city, Jerusalem. His heart was moved. A burden came upon him. Something had to happen. The situation had to change. The current condition was a disgrace to God and his people (Nehemiah 1:1-4; 2:3).

All positive change begins with seeing the need for that change first. As we take time to look at our world, look into God's Word,[28] look at other fruitful ministries and then look at our own churches, we can not help but see the need for change.

One of a leader's first tasks is to define reality. This is not being negative, it is being real. Unless we face the truth about the current situation we will never bring about the change that is needed. The good news is that every problem presents an opportunity.

The church needs to change. We need to move out of our comfort zones of tolerance with what currently exists. We need to become more relevant and more impacting as we seek to reach more people for Christ.

Change for change's sake is crazy, but change aimed at helping people and improving the effectiveness of the church is essential. Good leaders see the need for positive change in order to accomplish God's purposes and plans. Allow God to touch your heart with a fresh burden that motivates you to lead positive change.

2. RECEIVE A VISION FROM GOD

Nehemiah then spent time in prayer and waiting on God (see Nehemiah 1:4-11). He took the problem immediately to God, even though he had a natural bent for swift, decisive action. He positioned himself to hear from God. God showed him that he was to rebuild the walls of the city of Jerusalem. It was a big task, but it had to be done.

Over a period of time, Nehemiah allowed God to turn his burden into a vision. Bill Hybels defines vision as "a picture of the future that produces passion."[29] Vision is essential if we are to live motivated lives (Proverbs 29:18).

Every Christian and every leader needs to invest time into receiving a clear vision from God for their life and ministry. There is a big difference between vision and ambition. Ambition is what I want for my life. Vision is what God wants for my life and ministry.

Receiving a vision from God usually takes time. Have you ever taken a photo with a Polaroid camera? When the picture comes out, at first you do not see much at all. Then gradually the picture becomes clearer. In the same way, it takes time to see clearly what God has in mind for us and our future.

Allow God to birth his vision in you. Take time to dream. Think about what your church could look like. Nehemiah took four months to allow this process to move to completion. Only after that did he move to take action. In the same way, effective leaders tie all change to a clear vision and purpose. They know where they are headed and why.

3. CREATE A STRATEGIC PLAN

Nehemiah also put a good deal of time and effort into thinking through and developing a strategic plan that would make the vision a reality. He knew exactly *what* God wanted him to do (vision) and he had thought through all of the details of *how* he would do it (strategy). When asked by the king what he wanted, he was able to answer clearly and precisely. When asked how long it would take, he knew the exact time frame and he was also able to list the specific resources he would need to accomplish his task (Nehemiah 2:6-9).

The king asked specific questions and Nehemiah knew exactly what he wanted. Vagueness, at this point, would have shown up the project as a mere wish or sudden impulse. Nehemiah had prayed long enough and had enough faith to visualize the operation in some detail, even to the building technique he would use on the wall.

Once Nehemiah arrived in Jerusalem with the blessing of the king, he did further personal research to help him fine-tune his strategy (Nehemiah 2:11-16). He went and observed the actual areas that needed change. He did not just come up with some plan to solve an imaginary problem.

Accurate information is essential before you start making changes. As leaders, we must know and be fully aware of the state of our congregation (Proverbs 27:23) and then we must give attention to making positive change. Become involved at the grass roots level of the church and your local community. Observe, ask questions and listen really well. Take surveys, if necessary, and catch the pulse of the people.

Unfortunately, many church leaders do not take the time to plan as Nehemiah did. This needs to change because God is a great planner. He had a plan in creation as he formed the world. He broke this vision down into six bite-sized days of work. Then he rested on the seventh day of the week. Everything was done according to plan and within the estimated time frame. God also has a plan for redemption and he is working to accomplish it.

God gives visions to men and women and requires them to think and plan ahead. God gave Joseph a 14-year plan (Genesis 41:25-57). That was a long term forecast!

Wise leaders take their God-given vision and form it into a strategic plan that describes *how* and *when* the vision will become a reality. This takes time and involves a process. It requires wise and godly counsel from other people. The more significant the change, the more necessary it is to have input from all perspectives.

4. SPEAK TO THE INFLUENCERS

The first step Nehemiah took was to speak to the king. Without his blessing, the task would not even get underway (Nehemiah 2:3-6). The next action Nehemiah took was to go and talk to the Elders of Israel in the city of Jerusalem (Nehemiah 2:16-18). He did not go straight to the people and he did not begin doing the work himself. He realized that unless those who were in positions of influence bought into the vision, the change would not occur.

When speaking to the Elders, he did not present the solution first. He spoke to them about the problem so that they would agree on the need for change. Notice what he said. "You see the trouble we are in: Jerusalem lies in ruins, and its gates have been burned with fire. Come, let us rebuild the wall of Jerusalem, and we will no longer be in disgrace (Nehemiah 2:17)."

Unless people see and embrace the need for change, they will not be willing to pay the price or be committed to the work required to bring the change about. People need to understand the purpose of the change and see the benefits it will bring. Otherwise they will be unlikely to support the change initiative.

Wisdom teaches us that all change needs to be communicated and directed through the proper leadership channels and structures. We must influence the influencers. Understand the change process and the proper channels of authority and accountability. Work with this, not around it. Only when the key influencers are in unity can change occur without unnecessary damage.

Usually this takes a period of time. A good practice for any leadership team meetings is to make a distinction between matters of information, discussion and decision.

Major and far-reaching decisions should not usually be made in one meeting. It is far better to have extended times of discussion first (possibly in multiple meetings). Then when all perspectives have been considered and adequate time has been given for in-depth discussion, a decision can be made.

When people see the need for change and catch a realistic vision of how things could be better, they become motivated to become part of the solution. Be patient in this process so that you can move forward together. It is well worth it.

5. DEAL WITH OPPOSING FORCES

I wish I could tell you that there will be no problems when you lead change in the way we have been speaking about but the reality is that movement causes friction. Resistance to change is normal and so we need to prepare for it and handle it wisely. As soon as we start to make progress in God's work, we will know opposition.

Nehemiah faced (a) external opposition from those who were against the change. This opposition intensified as more and more progress was made (see Nehemiah 2:10, 19-20; 4:1-3, 7-8, 11-12; 6:1-14). It started with mild dislike and ended with outright aggressive attack.

In the same way, you will know what it is to face the onslaught of the enemy whenever you try to bring about positive change in the church. The devil hates the church and he especially targets churches that are a threat to his kingdom of darkness. You can be sure that you will experience a degree of spiritual warfare if you are advancing and taking ground for God.

Nehemiah countered this external attack with prayer (Nehemiah 4:4-5). He kept the people alert, awake and ready for battle at all times (Nehemiah 4:13-14, 16-23; 5:9, 19). His confidence was in God and he refused to be intimidated (Nehemiah 2:20).

In addition to the external attack, Nehemiah also encountered (b) internal problems during the change process. Times of transition are also times of vulnerability for any group of people. These internal conflicts had the potential to derail the entire project if they were not dealt with swiftly and effectively.

The first internal problem Nehemiah faced was discouragement. They were half way towards the completion of the project when the people felt like giving up (Nehemiah 4:6, 10). Maybe people were making comments such as, "Is it worth it?," "Is it really possible?" and "Whose idea was this anyway?" For some reason, they now doubted their power to complete the task. It was a natural sinking of heart. They were tired and discouraged. Nehemiah had to lift their morale and encourage them to finish the work that they had started. He reminded them that God was with them and that their very future was at stake (Nehemiah 4:14).

Many change initiatives in the church start out with a lot of enthusiasm, at least in those who initiated the change. But change is a process and it does not always happen as quickly and as smoothly as we would like it to. It is easy to become discouraged along the way and feel like giving up. However, we must remember the urgent need for the change and embrace the vision God has given us once again.

The next internal problem Nehemiah faced was conflict (Nehemiah 5:1-13). He immediately went to work bringing resolution to the situation. This required acquiring all of the facts by listening to everyone involved in the conflict.

Notice the different stories that were being given by the different groups of people. Each group had a completely different story, depending on their perspective of the situation (Nehemiah 5:1-5). Nehemiah was very angry, but he first pondered everything carefully, then confronted in love (Nehemiah 5:6-11). In his response, he controlled his emotions, choosing wisely to not deal with the problem while he was angry. He then directly confronted those who were wrong, giving them the right action that needed to be taken.

As we lead change, there may be conflicts that emerge. It is vital that we resolve them quickly and thoroughly. We should not ignore them. It is wise to gather all the facts and to never confront when you are angry. We must learn the balance of having the *courage* to confront the issues and the *consideration* to do so in a loving manner (Ephesians 4:15. 2 Timothy 2:24-26). We must speak the truth in love and practice loving confrontation.

In every change, there will be opposing forces. Someone or something will face loss, despite any potential gains. Letting go of the old can be extremely difficult and until people have taken hold of the new, the in-between time can feel a little like a trapeze artist must feel hanging in mid-air. You may encounter anger, frustration, fear, uncertainty and disappointment during the transition. Realize that this is normal! Wise leaders think through the possible reactions or problems and avoid unnecessary conflict by preparing for and addressing these forces in advance.

William Bridges says, "It isn't the changes that do you in, it's the transitions."[30] It is one thing to get Israel out of Egypt. It is another thing to get them through the wilderness and into the Promised Land.

LEADING CHANGE

Nehemiah led the people of Israel to finish the work in exactly fifty-two days (Nehemiah 6:15-16). He saw the need for change, he received a clear vision from God, he translated that vision into a strategic plan, he managed to bring all of the influencers into agreement, and he dealt with the opposing forces along the way. He worked hard and he refused to give up. He finished! He was a man with a vision who made it a reality.

There is a great sense of joy and fulfilment that comes when you are able to bring about positive change. It requires God's help and a great deal of patient endurance on the part of the leader. However, if the vision is from God, it is well worth the effort. Avoid continually changing direction. Yes, make adjustments along the way, but finish what you start. Commit to it and be willing to pay the price.

APPLYING THE PROCESS

I have used this process of leading change continually for well over fifteen years of church leadership. It really works. It works for starting new ministries, closing down old or ineffective ministries, changing church culture and values, changing long held traditions, making staff changes, restructuring ministries, and changing policies. Any change worth making will benefit from a well-thought out change process such as this.

Just remember, no matter how well you lead change and how well-planned your process is, there will be opposing forces. During periods of major change, we have experienced tension, disagreements, letters of criticism, and even some people leaving the church. However, we have done our best to handle all of these situations with as much grace and wisdom as possible. You too will need to anticipate opposing forces and then seek to handle them with courage, wisdom and grace.

Jesus once told this interesting parable: "No one tears a patch from a new garment and sews it on an old one. If he does, he will have torn the new garment, and the patch from the new will not match the old. And no one pours new wine into old wineskins. If he does, the new wine will burst the skins, the wine will run out and the wineskins will be ruined. No, new wine must be poured into new wineskins. And no one after drinking old wine wants the new, for he says, 'The old is better (Luke 5:36-39).'"

Every church has it's *old* ones (not necessarily in age) who are used to the old wine and believe that the old way of doing things is better. They were probably in the church before the changes were made and they may find it difficult to adjust to the new way of doing things. This is natural as all change takes time to process. The *new* ones who come in after the change usually love the new because that is all they know.

The challenge is to continue to provide new wine and wean those old ones on to it. Even Jesus said, "No one, having drunk old wine, immediately desires new; for he says, 'The old is better.'" In the process, mixing in a little old wine may be wise. Jesus also said, "Therefore every scribe instructed concerning the kingdom of heaven is like a householder who brings out of his treasure things new and old (Matthew 13:52 NKJV)."

Making sudden, radical or revolutionary change, although sometimes necessary, will usually cause a reaction. Gradual evolutionary change often works much better as it enables people to adjust over a period of time. Both types of change have their strengths and weaknesses, and may be appropriate for different situations.

Also, understand that different people respond differently to change. Innovators and dreamers love change and seek to constantly create it. Other people know a good idea when they see it and embrace the change once they are given time to understand it. Some people naturally tend to be more hesitant and sceptical. Avoid rebuking them. Take time to talk with them and hear their concerns. Often, you will gain further insight from them into how to make the change more successful and you will give them the chance to hear your heart and the motivation for the change. Some people may not ever embrace some changes.

Once you turn the church, which may be likened to a bus, in a new direction or on a different route, some people will inevitably get off to join another bus going in a direction they want to go. You have to be prepared for this, although keeping as many with you as possible is the aim. Also, people differ in their response depending on the issue. It depends on how a particular change affects them.

It is essential that you know in your own spirit that God is leading you and that you are moving out in his will for your ministry and your church. The giants will be there and the need for courage will be great. However, as you seek God, he will guide you and give you wisdom and favour with the people.

Change is not easy. In fact, it can be very uncomfortable. However, the church must change if it is to be what God intends it to be in the world. Lead your church boldly through change focused at bringing about the purposes of God in your local community.

REFLECTION QUESTIONS

1. Reflect on some changes that you have *led* in the past? What went well and what didn't? What are some lessons you can learn for future initiatives?

2. Reflect on some changes that you have *observed* in the past? What went well and what didn't? What are some lessons you can learn for future initiatives?

3. Consider the leader's role as *change agent*. Why is change management such a neglected area of training within churches and even seminaries?

4. Think of a change that has taken place where *what* was being changed was good and positive but *how* it was changed (the process) ended up hijacking the effectiveness of the change. What could have been done better?

5. Make a list of three changes that you would like to make in your church or ministry in the coming six months. Next, take time to plan each potential change through the suggested process of change by answering these questions:

    a. Why do you think the change is needed?

    b. What is your vision of a better future?

    c. What is your plan for making the change?

    d. Who are the influencers you will speak to?

    e. What are the potential opposing forces?

6. Further developing question #5, how could you prepare in advance to respond to any opposing forces?

Closing Words

Leadership transition is a critical time in the life of any church, ministry or organization. When it is done well, everyone benefits and the mission can continue to unfold from generation to generation. When it is done poorly or not at all, everyone loses and the mission is often aborted. That is why it is so important to go about it wisely.

I urge you to prepare for the future by thinking about passing the baton. At some time and at some stage in your life and ministry you will probably have the opportunity to transition to a successor. Determine ahead of time to do it well.

Remember that ultimately it is not just about you. It is about others and the work of God here on earth. Our transitions are not just about Richard, my dad and me. It is about the church of Jesus Christ and its ability to carry out its purpose in the world.

Closing Words

Because of good transitions we have a congregation that is blessed, healthy, growing and passionately pursuing its mission to "impact communities, cities and nations for the kingdom of God." More people are coming to Christ all the time, disciples are being trained, believers are being mobilised into ministry, leaders are being equipped, new ministries are being launched and new congregations are being started. That is God's intentions for every local church.

We will each be rewarded for the work that we do but our greatest joy should be to see the church of Jesus rise and make a difference in our time. Let's be people who are excited about releasing others into ministry. Then let's cheer them on to even greater things than we have ever seen before.

I pray that what we have shared in this book has been an inspiration and an encouragement to you. I hope that you will have found some of the lessons and principles from our journey helpful to your own ministry context. Heaven and earth are cheering you on.

REFLECTION QUESTIONS

1. Imagine your life and ministry at the age of 75. What will you be doing and what legacy would you have liked to have left by that time?

2. What are the requirements for your current ministry role in terms of character (what a person must *be*), knowledge (what a person must *know*) and ministry skills (what a person must be able to *do*)?

3. Who are the potential replacements for your current ministry role? What areas do they need to develop the most in order to be ready to receive the baton of ministry or leadership?

4. What could you do in terms of apprenticing, coaching or training to help develop their potential for this possible transition?

5. Who are some older and more experienced mentors who you could learn from as you seek to effectively pass the baton some time in the future?

6. Once you are no longer in your current ministry role, where else could you make a contribution?

7. What skills and interests outside your current ministry role could you begin to develop now?

8. Read Bob Buford's book *Halftime* and complete the exercises.[33]

9. What three principles or ideas from this book could you apply immediately?

Frequently Asked Questions

1. "How do you all get along?"

Richard and Kevin have been friends since 1951. Although different in personality they have always shared a common love for God and for his Word. They also have been passionate about seeing the church arise to be all God intends for it to be.

Kevin and Richard have continued to attend our church when they have been around. They both have provided support and encouragement to me. I have also caught up with them personally from time to time. There has been a genuine sense of friendship between us all.

2. "Do you think that other previous senior ministers can stay in their church successfully or has this just been a unique thing at CityLife Church?"

There is no doubt that in many situations the normal thing to do is for the previous leader to leave for another place and have no contact and nothing to do with his or her former congregation. Most ministers leave for another city and take over another congregation or move into a different ministry environment. This frees everyone involved from any potential tensions that could arise.

However, sometimes leaving is not an option for the previous senior minister, especially if they have no relationships outside the church or other ministry opportunities. I do believe it is possible for a previous senior minister to stay in the same church. It just requires some very good relationships, maturity of character and ongoing honest communication about matters that will inevitably arise. If there is the appropriate letting go and honour that we spoke about earlier, then a workable relationship really is achievable.

3. "If the previous senior minister stays in the church, is it necessary for the outgoing senior minister to be away for a period of time after the hand over?"

This is definitely the wisest thing to do, in my opinion, as it is such an important time. I would recommend at least three months. Richard went on a nine week ministry trip after my dad became the senior minister and then he travelled a fair amount in the ensuing years. My father travelled away after I became the senior minister and he was involved in outside ministry for the best part of a year. Since that time he has continued to have an active itinerant ministry.

The purpose of this period of time is to help the previous leader to appropriately disengage from their ministry role. Often this can be a somewhat emotional time and there is a natural sense of grieving which happens any time there is a loss. This time also provides the new leader some space to begin leading without the sense of someone looking over their shoulder.

4. "Do the previous senior ministers ever preach?"

It is important that the new senior minister becomes the primary feeder of the congregation and that the congregation is appropriately weaned off a dependence on the outgoing senior minister. It is also important that the new leader develop a teaching team over time. This includes training and releasing others into preaching ministry.

When my dad took over from Richard, he still had Richard speak from time to time but less so as time went on. I have done the same with my dad. Obviously, the senior minister should initiate any invitation to speak.

At this stage in the life of our church, my father teaches from time to time in the various training programs of our church. He is an outstanding Bible teacher and people are always blessed by his insights. He also occasionally visits various Life Groups, often for question and answer times on theological matters.

5. "We are training up a younger leader as a potential future senior minister. What advice would you give us?"

Ideally, a senior minister should be somewhat of an all-rounder who has had a reasonable amount of experience in a number of the major areas of church life. This may include areas such as children's ministry, youth, worship, administration, and pastoral care. Of course, previous involvement in each of these ministries is not necessary. However, there is no doubt that my effectiveness as a senior minister has been greatly influenced by my previous ten years of involvement as a church staff member in a variety of other ministries.

In addition to a close personal relationship with God and godly character, some important skills and abilities to develop are (a) *leadership ability*, which includes the ability to set vision, lead teams, train leaders and make things happen, and (b) *communication ability*. The senior minister is the primary feeder of the congregation and therefore must be able to have the ability to prepare relevant messages on a diverse range of subjects. This does not mean that he or she has to preach/teach every week but they must be gifted to carry the major load of communication. Because of this, a good theological education is extremely helpful. Healthy growing churches are led well and fed well. Senior ministers need to be able to do both with excellence.

To help a potential leader come to the place where they are confident that God has called them to this position, I would encourage you to send them to connect with some senior ministers who are leading churches a bit larger than your own. This will help them discover what it feels like to lead a church your size and what spiritual gifts are required. This process will allow God to confirm to them whether this is really the right step for them or not.

6. "What is the role of the senior minister's spouse?"

If a senior minister is married, it is important that their spouse be supportive of them and that they endeavour to provide a godly example to the congregation. When it comes to ministry, they should simply do what they are gifted to do and what they are passionate about. There is no set mould that has to be followed.

Richard's wife, Margaret (affectionately known as Garry) had a gift of hospitality which she used to bless many. Other than that she was not actively involved in other major ministries within the church. My mother, Joyce Conner, had teaching and pastoral gifts so was active in leading the women's ministries of the church along with supporting my father in his leadership role. My dad's second wife, Rene, has also been active in ministry for many years, including preaching and counselling.

Before I became the senior minister, my wife, Nicole, helped me lead the church's youth ministry for five years. When I first became the senior minister, our children were quite young so Nicole was less involved in church ministry at that time. Over the years, Nicole has become increasingly involved and now she is on part time staff, overseeing our women's ministries and she is part of our teaching team and our senior leadership team.

The above comments also apply to a woman if she is the senior minister and to her husband (the spouse in that case). Someone once said that the pastor's spouse is possibly the most neglected person in any congregation. It is a unique role and adequate attention needs to be given to thinking it through so as to create realistic and clear expectations for all involved.

7. "Is it wise to pass on leadership to a family member?"

There is great danger in showing favoritism to anyone in a church leadership situation, including family members. Leaders should be chosen based on their individual calling, character and competency – not who they know or who they are related to. Promoting friends or family members into leadership positions they are not qualified for is an abuse of the leadership office and will only cause damage to the health of the church and the credibility of the leadership. However, the fact that someone is a family member or friend should not disqualify them from being considered for leadership if they clearly have what it takes.

In our situation, my dad and the elders chose me as the next senior minister not because I was related to my dad. It was because they saw God's hand on my life for this leadership role. This is essential. The people must feel secure in the process. Otherwise they will vote with their feet by potentially leaving the church.

8. "Could you explain a bit more about the two year transition time between you and your father's leadership?"

As I mentioned, during this time I began taking responsibility for the day-to-day running of the church. This included leading staff meetings, overseeing church meetings, preaching more, employing staff, overseeing the church's pastoral ministries and providing some leadership training. By the end of this period, I was beginning to form vision and strategic plans for the coming years.

By the way, if a prospective senior minister has been the youth pastor, I think it is important to wean people from this narrow perception by having them involved in a wider range of adult ministries so that the whole church will learn to embrace them.

Our two year transition time was ideal. The key is to not make it too short (if possible) or too long. The right time is usually determined by the readiness of the two senior ministers (current and future), as well as the congregation.

9. "What were the financial arrangements for the previous senior ministers?"

When Richard stepped down as the senior minister, the Board of Elders decided to give him 100% of his salary for the rest of his life. This decision was made for a number of reasons: the fact that Richard had poured twenty years of his life into the church (many of those as a volunteer), the fact that he had not been paid any social security or superannuation during that time, and because they wanted to honour him as the founding pastor. Richard remained an elder but was no longer on staff. He moved his office to his home immediately after my dad became the senior minister.

When my father stepped down as senior minister, the Board of Elders decided to give him 75% of his salary for the rest of his life due to the fact that he had not been paid any social security or superannuation during his early years on staff. My dad had been senior minister for only eight years, in contrast to Richard's twenty, but there was still a desire to honour him for his significant contribution to the church.

My dad remained an elder and also stayed on staff but in a new role. He continued to do this for a number of years until his role shifted to a greater focus outside the church (with travelling ministry, book writing and leading his minister's fellowship). My dad has worked from home for the last number of years (mainly because we are out of office space for our other staff ministries).

I can honestly say that I believe God has blessed our church for treating our previous senior ministers well financially. Each situation is unique and where there has been adequate retirement provision, ongoing salary will most likely be unnecessary. However, the principle is to honour those who have laboured diligently in ministry over so many years.

10. "You mention that both Richard and your father have stayed on the eldership team. How has this worked out and do you recommend it?"

In many situations, the previous senior minister would not stay on the Board of Elders once they have stepped down from that role. There are a number of benefits in this approach, both for them and the new senior minister.

In our situation, it seemed best to provide some ongoing continuity and we were able to do this successfully because of our good relationships. I would honestly say that having both Richard and my father still as elders for a season caused me to move a little more slowly with certain changes. But overall, I would say it has helped me be a wiser leader.

However, there is no doubt that this situation does create a unique dynamic that has to be handled with care. If not, then tension can easily emerge that could potentially damage the unity of the leadership team. This is especially true when changes are being made that the previous senior minister may not agree with or would not have made. I would simply say that any previous senior minister needs to be able to handle change well and the current senior minister needs both grace and patience during any change process.

We have had our share of disagreements but thankfully we have been able to focus on the various issues at hand and not let this affect our personal relationships. This has given us the foundation to work through issues until they are resolved.

Out of courtesy to both Richard and my father, if there was a major change I was about to suggest that I knew they would probably be unhappy with, I would try to speak to them personally about it before they heard it at an elders meeting. I would explain why I was suggesting the change and I would express my understanding that they might not agree. By taking this high road I often found them understanding and in many cases supportive of the change. I consider this as simply speaking to the influencers, which is a wise part of leading any change.

I should note that a few years ago we conducted a church-wide governance review. This resulted in a rewrite of our constitution, the formation of a new Policy Governance Manual, and some changes to the membership of our Board of Elders' team. Richard and my father ceased being elders at that time although they continued to be available for advice and support as required. This change was not due to any problems with their involvement but it was simply part of a further passing of the baton to the next generation of leaders.[31]

11. "What should the previous senior minister do if congregation members approach them with concerns about the church?"

This will inevitably happen when a previous senior minister stays in the church. How they handle these types of situations will have a major impact on the unity and therefore the health of the church. It is a highly sensitive area.

The appropriate way to handle any criticism or complaints is for the former senior minister to ask that person to go and speak to the new senior minister or another member of the leadership team. This is part of letting go properly and of realizing that you are no longer in the senior role of responsibility. I am thankful that both Richard and my father have handled themselves well in these types of situations. This is a credit to their maturity. If there have been doubts or rumors, I have spoken directly to them in person about it and you will need to do the same in your situation lest division begin to occur.

For the current senior minister, it is wise to keep relationship with the previous senior minister and be open to listening to any feedback they may have or may be receiving. The dynamics of any church are such that many people do not go directly to the senior leader when they have concerns. They often go to someone else on the leadership team and therefore you need to see their feedback as helpful rather than destructive. They can be your ears and help to keep you aware of things happening within the church that you need to know about.

12. "As a new senior minister, how long does it take until the church you've inherited feels like yours?"

This is a very good question. Not long after becoming the senior minister I read a book on church leadership that said it takes about seven years before you feel like the church is yours. I thought, "No way!" But as time has gone on, I have found out that it really does take a while.

The difference between inheriting a church and planting a church is similar to the difference between adopting a child and having your own child. When you adopt a child it already has certain tendencies, habits and DNA. Some of these are good and need to be encouraged while others need some reshaping. In many ways, it is like that when you inherit a church that someone else founded or led.

When you first take the role of senior minister, 100% of the people came in under someone else's leadership. The people younger than you will most likely gravitate to your leadership right away while the older ones may need some time before they give you their full trust and support. Avoid reacting to this but reach out to them in love and consideration. Over time you can win them over.

Eventually, if your church is growing, a greater and greater percentage of the congregation will have come in after you became the senior minister. Your leadership will be all that they have known and you will feel more and more that you have the reins of the church.[32]

When previous senior ministers are still around, there may be a sense that you are still under their shadow. Do your best to not be intimidated by this. Allow people to honour and respect them. Focus on developing yourself and being the best you can be. Over time you will make your own shadow and God will use you to advance his kingdom.

13. "At what age should a senior minister begin thinking about passing the baton to a successor?"

There is no set time or ideal age for this. Each person and each situation is unique. The key thing is to do what is best for the church and its ongoing health and growth. Ideally you want to make the transition at the peak of your ministry effectiveness rather than holding on for too long and then seeing the church begin to plateau or decline.

No matter what your age, now is the time to begin thinking about your future and a succession plan. It is also wise to begin developing multiple ministry pathways so that, once your time comes to pass the baton to another senior minister, you have a variety of other ministry contributions to make in the latter part of your life.

Frequently Asked Questions

My dad passed the baton of church leadership to me at the age of sixty-eight and he has probably been busier in ministry over the last decade or so than he was before. Then again, he has amazing capacity. I tell people he has an every ready battery.

Even at the age of fifty, if you have your health, you have the potential of another thirty or more years of productive ministry. Do not see this as a season to retire but as a time to re-fire for a new assignment. As Bob Buford says in his best selling book *Halftime*, in the second half of our life we need to shift our focus from success to significance.[33]

Recommended Reading

Following are a number of books that you may find helpful:

1. *Transforming Your Church* by Mark Conner (Conner Ministries Inc: Melbourne, Australia, 2010). In this book I outline seven strategic changes that every church must make. These are biblical principles for building a healthy and growing church in whatever context. In the USA, this material is published under the title *Seven Strategic Changes Every Church Must Make* (City Christian Publishing: Portland, Oregon, 2006).
2. *Successful Christian Ministry* by Mark Conner (Conner Ministries Inc: Melbourne, Australia, 2003). In this practical book I share seven principles for having a high impact and long lasting ministry. It contains excellent material for training church staff, leaders or volunteers.

Recommended Reading

3. *Managing Transitions – Making the Most of Change* by William Bridges (Da Capo Press: Philadelphia, PA, 2009). This is one of the best books on leading change available. It has a special emphasis on understanding the emotional aspects of transitions. Highly recommended reading, The checklists at the end of each chapter are worth the price of the book.

4. *Leading Change* by John P. Kotter (Harvard Business School Press: Boston, MA, 1996). This is a classic business book on leading change. I read this a few years after I had put together a process for leading change from the life of Nehemiah. I was interested at the similarities between these and the change process shared in this book. God's Word never ceases to amaze me as to its relevance to our contemporary world. There is nothing you will read that God did not think of first – because he is the best leader!

5. *The Heart of Change* by John P. Kotter and Dan S. Cohen (Harvard Business School Press: Boston, MA, 2002). In this follow up book to *Leading Change*, John Kotter shares real life examples of his model for leading change from a number of organisations.

6. *How to Change Your Church without Killing It* by Alan Nelson and Gene Appel (WORD Publishing Group: Nashville, TN, 2000). This book has a great deal of wisdom and insight on leading change within a church context from two experienced Christian leaders.

7. *The Church in the New Testament* by Kevin J. Conner (City Christian Publishing: Portland, Oregon, 1998). This is an excellent textbook on the

theology of the church, gleaned from years of study of the New Testament.

8. *From an Acorn to an Oak Tree* by Richard Holland (Richard Holland: Melbourne, Australia, 1999). This small booklet outlines some of the early days and history of CityLife Church (formerly Waverley Christian Fellowship).

Postscript

February 2017 was a big month for CityLife Church. Over three successive weekends, it celebrated it's 50th anniversary as a church, farwelled Mark Conner after 32 years on staff, and inducted Andrew Hill as its fourth Senior Minister.

Mark led the church as its Senior Minister for over 22 years, seeing the congregation grow to around 10,000 people meeting in 11 weekend church services in four locations across the city of Melbourne. As a result of prayer and conversations in 2015, he and the Elders felt it was time for a change, both for him and the church. This led to a search process, considering both internal and external candidates, and the eventual selection of Andrew Hill as the next Senior Minister. A time of transition then took place as Mark endeavoured to pass on to Andrew as much as he could in order to help him prepare for his new role.

Postscript

After taking a few months off, Mark is now giving himself to helping the wider church through speaking, writing, coaching and mentoring. For more information or to contact Mark visit his web site at www.markconner.com.au. Mark's prayer is that CityLife Church continues to go from strength to strength under its new leadership.

NOTES

1. A revised edition of this book was published recently in Australia (Conner Ministries Inc.: Melbourne, Australia, 2010). This book has also been published in the USA by City Christian Publishing (Portland, Oregon, 2006). In addition, it has been translated into Swedish, Russian and Indonesian.

2. Wendell Smith's book, *Pastoring Youth in a New Generation* (City Bible Publishing; Portland, Oregon, 1987), further outlines these generation purposes. Unfortunately this book is no longer in print. Wendell is founding pastor of The City Church in Seattle, Washington (see www.thecity.org).

3. These two shifts are fully explained in my book, *Transforming Your Church*, along with many practical examples of how to apply them personally and in your church.

4. Our family was part of Waverley Mission from the very early years. I attended Sunday School classes there as a child. However, in 1972 our family relocated to Portland, Oregon where my dad, Kevin Conner, assisted Dick Iverson with the leadership of Portland Bible College and what was then known as Bible Temple (now called City Bible Church, and led since 1995 by my brother-in-law and sister, Frank and Sharon Damazio). We stayed in the USA for ten years. Then in 1981, my parents and I returned to Melbourne where we resumed connection with Waverley Mission (renamed Waverley Christian Fellowship at that time).

5. For a more detailed description of the growth and development of Waverley Christian Fellowship during the twenty years of Richard Holland's leadership, see his booklet *From an Acorn to an Oak Tree*.

6. My mother, Joyce Conner, had a heart attack and passed away very suddenly in 1990. It was a time of great grief for our family and our church. Two years later my dad married Rene Arrowsmith who had been a friend of the family for many years and was actively involved in the church at that time. They have been happily married ever since.

Notes

7   Numbers are helpful because they provide objective "vital signs" for measuring the health and growth of a church. On the other hand, numbers can be very impersonal – that's why we try not to over-emphasise or overuse them. However, each number represents a person that matters to God.

8   These documents can be viewed at www.citylifechurch.com

9   In August 2010, we have a record of 9,379 people who are part of our church family and involved in our church each month. However, not all these people attend every weekend, hence our lower average weekly attendance. For information about the multi-site model, visit www.blog.markconner.com.au and search the "church" category of posts.

10 In August 2010, 60% of our 9,394 people were involved in a Life Group.

11 Our LIFETRAX course manuals for teachers and students can be ordered online at our web site.

12 Illustration from the article *Heir Apparent* by Skye Jethani in the Fall 2005 edition of *Leadership Journal* (Published by Christianity Today International: Carol Stream, IL), p.51.

13 *Built to Last: Successful Habits of Visionary Companies* by James C. Collins and Jerry I. Porras (HarperCollins Publishers: New York, NY, 1994).

14 The book *The Leadership Pipeline* by Ram Charan, Stephen Drotter and James Noel (Jossey-Bass: San Francisco, CA, 2001) is an excellent book on leadership development.

15 From February 2005 edition of *Harvard Business Review* (Harvard Business Publishing Company: Boston, MA).

16 ibid.

17 From November 2004 edition of *Harvard Business Review* (Harvard Business Publishing Company: Boston, MA).

18 My dad's auto-biography is called *This Is My Story*, (KJC Ministries: Melbourne, Australia, 2007). Many people have read his textbooks on various biblical and doctrinal subjects.

	Now you have the opportunity to learn many important lessons from his life journey. See also www.kevinconner.org
19	A special thanks to my dad for providing this illustration.
20	Charles Ridley, a social scientist, has developed an excellent list of thirteen qualities that are essential for any potential church planter. These are also very applicable to selecting leaders for existing churches. For further information, see the http://www.churchplanting4me.org/ridleyfactors.htm
21	Jesus did this incredibly well. He gave his disciples a clear mission and he outlined values for his kingdom. He then left his enterprise, the church, in the hands of his disciples, who were to carry it forward until his return. All enduring organizations are built around a strong sense of mission, not the personality of one leader.
22	The likelihood of a successor desiring to totally change a church and lead it in a different direction is often greater when the successor is from the outside.
23	My dad was keen for me to take the leadership of the church a number of years earlier than this but Nicole and I did not feel it was the right step for us at the time. My dad did not pressure us but a number of years later we all sensed it was God's will and God's time for this transition to take place.
24	An inauguration service is a special time when the new leader is commissioned to their leadership position. This is an important time for the previous leader, the new leader and the congregation as it clearly marks the transition of leadership (for a biblical example, see Numbers 27:15-23).
25	A church that does not change or make transitions can tend to fossilize. My dad defines a fossil as "a living creature that failed to make the transition."
26	Read about these in detail in *Transforming Your Church*.
27	For a full outline of principles for leading change from Nehemiah's life, see the chapter on "Leading Change" in *Transforming Your Church*.

Notes

28   One important key to leading change effectively is to build all change upon biblical principles, if at all possible. Once people see the foundation for the change in the Scriptures and know why the change is needed, it is far more likely that they will accept and work with a particular change. This provides a sense of safety and security.

29   *Courageous Leadership* by Bill Hybels (Zondervan Publishing House: Grand Rapids, Michigan, 2002), p.32.

30   See his excellent book *Managing Transitions: Making the Most of Change* (Da Capo Press: Philadelphia, PA, 2009), p.3.

31   See my blog (www.blog.markconner.com.au) under the "Church" or "Leadership" category for an overview of our governance review and an outline of the changes that we made, as well as a list of helpful resources related to this important aspect of church life.

32   For a full outline of this concept, see chapter 10 of *Leading and Managing Your Church* by Carl F. George and Robert E. Logan (Fleming H. Revell Company: Old Tappan, New Jersey, 1987).

33   *Halftime* by Bob Buford (Zondervan Publishing House: Grand Rapids, Michigan, 1994). I would highly recommend this book to any leader who is over forty years of age as it will give them a proper perspective on the rest of their life. Buford's subsequent books *Game Plan* and *Stuck in Halftime* are also worth reading.

TRANSFORMING YOUR CHURCH
SEVEN STRATEGIC SHIFTS

If there was ever a need for a healthy, relevant and dynamic churches to emerge, it's right now In today's culture of constant change, how is it possible for a church to remain relevant and effective? In this book, Mark Conner reveals seven strategic shifts that every church must make in order to be effective in the 21st century.

These principles will help your church play a vital role in extending the kingdom of God to impact communities, cities and nations for his glory.

"Mark Conner is a superb leader and communicator whose vision has led to remarkable growth in his own church. I am so grateful for his friendship and inspiring example."

Nicky Gumbel Vicar of Holy Trinity Brompton and Developer of ALPHA International

SUCCESSFUL CHRISTIAN MINISTRY

The Bible teaches that every Christian is a minister. In fact, the church needs more ministers not just more members. Only as every believer discovers their spiritual gifts and begins to serve passionately will we see the church rise up to fulfill its destiny to take the gospel to the nations and be salt and light in each local community. If there ever was a time for every Christian to rise up and take their place in effective ministry, it's right now.

What are the keys to building a high impact long lasting ministry? In this book, Mark Conner shares seven principles for building a successful Christian ministry drawn from his years of ministry experience and observation. Each chapter is packed with practical advice that will empower you to reach your God-given potential and to make a positive difference in the lives of other people.

Available in paperback format from www.word.com.au and in paperback and eBook format from www.amazon.com/author/markconner

PRISON BREAK
FINDING PERSONAL FREEDOM

Living in our broken world creates the possibility of becoming trapped by various negative emotions and habits that can easily become like a prison around us. In this helpful book, Mark Conner shares practical principles for finding freedom from common problems such as anger, fear, worry, rejection, depression, addictions, and spiritual bondages. With God's help you can make a prison break - beginning today.

"The book is practical yet sound, both psychologically and biblically and easy to read. I am sure no reader will be disappointed."
Archibald D. Hart. Fuller Theological Seminary

Available in paperback format from www.word.com.au and in paperback and eBook format fromwww.amazon.com/author/markconner

THE SPIRITUAL JOURNEY
UNDERSTANDING THE STAGES OF FAITH

When you are on a journey, it helps to have a map of the terrain and a guide to help you along the way. In this book, Mark Conner presents such a map and guides us through the stages of faith that are common to the spiritual journey. This journey is rarely linear or in a straight line. There are many curves, twists and surprises along the way. Sometimes we seem to move in circles or in random patterns that don't make sense at the time. Nevertheless, God is at work in our lives. Welcome to the journey of faith.

"Christians throughout the world are asking themselves what lifelong discipleship really means in today's fast-changing culture. Mark Conner has written a thoughtful guide, combining his own personal experience with insightful Biblical and theological reflection – all of it offering practical ways to live as faithful followers of Jesus."
John Drane
UK Theologian and Best-Selling Author.

Available in paperback format from www.word.com.au and in paperback and eBook format fromwww.amazon.com/author/markconner

MONEY TALKS
PRINCIPLES FOR FINANCIAL FREEDOM

Australia is one of the richest countries in the world yet, despite this fact, many people are under financial pressure. In this book, Mark Conner shares practical principles for becoming financially free and living wisely with the resources we have. Learn fresh insights about earning, saving, investing, debt reduction and spending wisely. The book also includes extra material on church finances, fundraising and the purpose of business.

"Countless books on how to use money compete for readers. It is easy to find complicated ones. It is common to find those that just promote getting rich, even by so-called Christians. There are plenty of theoretical studies that are hard to apply and how-to-manuals not based in good theory. But where does one find a short, practical, biblically grounded, clearly written little book that addresses all the important questions about using money in Christian ways with up-to-date charts, graphs and statistics to back everything up? Mark Conner has now written it. Get a copy. Devour it. Then live it out."

Craig L. Blomberg
Distinguished Professor of New Testament. Denver Seminary.

Available in paperback format from www.word.com.au and in paperback and eBook format www.amazon.com/author/markconner

HOW TO AVOID BURNOUT
FIVE HABITS OF HEALTHY LIVING

In a world of rapid change, growing complexity and increasing pressure, stress and burnout are becoming common place. In this practical book, Mark Conner shares five habits for healthy living, gleaned from his decades of experience as an organizational leader and Christian minister.

"This book is both timely and important. My 14 years of mentoring a wide range of Christian leaders has convinced me that emotional depletion is widespread and at almost epidemic proportions. If anyone is qualified to write this book it is Mark Conner. He is a long term outstandingly gifted leader with a huge emotional tank who has been very honest about his own journey. The book is well researched and written with very practical guidelines and a rich set of biblical and other references."

Keith Farmer, B.Comm.,B.A.(Hons),D.Min.
Former Principal of Australian College of Ministries

Available in paperback format from www.word.com.au and in paperback and eBook format from www.amazon.com/author/markconner

EVERYDAY EXPERIENCES OF THE DIVINE

Life moves quickly, and it's easy to miss the sacred moments that are woven into our ordinary days. In *Everyday Experiences of the Divine*, Mark Conner invites you to slow down, breathe a little deeper, and notice where God might already be at work - in conversations, in nature, in times of change, and in the quiet, in-between spaces of life.

Through personal stories, Scripture, and gentle reflection, Mark explores how God meets us. Not just in the big or dramatic moments, but in the small and surprising ones that fill our everyday lives.

This isn't a book about escaping life, but about entering it more deeply. It's an invitation to live awake - to see grace in the familiar, wisdom in the waiting, and beauty in the flow of each new day.

If you've ever longed for a faith that feels real and grounded, one that makes sense of both joy and struggle, this book will help you recognise God's quiet presence in it all.

www.ingramcontent.com/pod-product-compliance
Lightning Source LLC
Chambersburg PA
CBHW020448220526
45464CB00002B/904